Some Observations of a Stranger at Zuni in the Latter Part of the Century

Other books by Clarence Major

Fiction

All Night Visitors
No
Reflex and Bone Structure
Emergency Exit
My Amputations
Such Was the Season
Painted Turtle: Woman with Guitar

Poetry

The Fires That Burn in Heaven
Love Poems of a Black Man
Human Juices
Swallow the Lake
Symptoms & Madness
Private Line
The Cotton Club
The Syncopated Cakewalk
Inside Diameter: The France Poems

Some Observations

of a Stranger at Zuni

in the Latter Part

of the Century

Clarence Major

Cover design: Katie Messborn

Some of these poems originally appeared in the following maga-
zines: *Callalo* ("In Hollywood with the Zuni God of War); *Exquisite
Corpse* ("Sign Language"); *Hambone* ("A Gallup Swill-Hole or, Can-
tina Blues" and "Tewa Victories") and *In Their Own Words* ("Some
Observations of a Stranger at Zuni in the Latter Part of the
Century").

Publication of this book was made possible, in part, through a match-
ing grant from the California Arts Council and through contribu-
tions to The Contemporary Arts Educational Project, Inc.

Library of Congress Cataloguing in Publication Data

Major, Clarence

    Some Observations of a Stranger at Zuni in the
    Latter Part of the Century

    I. Title

ISBN: 1-55713-020-5

FIRST EDITION

5   4   3   2   1

New American Poetry Series: No. 2 N(2)A
                                  P

Sun & Moon Press
6148 Wilshire Boulevard
Gertrude Stein Plaza
Los Angeles, CA 90048

Introductory Note

These poems were inspired by spending time at Zuni and by living with the spirit and history of the Zunis and with the spirits of Southwestern Indians. They also, in a way, come out of my memory of my grandparents telling of the Indians among our own ancestors in the Southeast.

I wish to thank the Fellowship Council on Research and Creative Work, Graduate School, University of Colorado at Boulder, for the generous grant which made the writing of this book possible.

Contents

Lost in the Desert

I

The sun,
        in her memory,
                        held itself high
above its bed,
        the mountains—to the South.
Human bone, beaded dolls, chunks
                        of turquoise,
were the relics of her cove.
The "Coral direction" pleased her,
            looking down that range
to the sound of tesese (once she
                tapped the taut skin
    herself and heard the power of
                            sound
lift up from the orifice).

Her throat dried faster than the pit
    of a clay oven when
                    the match is
    struck to paper
                beneath the wood.
In silence, she turned
                her small emery wheel.
In silence, in silence.
The sun
        disappeared
behind the range like a prairie wolf
entering
        a path through desert rock.

She was out
                    here now (in the music).
Her heart was a terrified cactus wren
          gripped
in a dirty fist.
                    Unseen Hands was not there
to protect her
          from the Mystery—
                    and its danger:
he's a gray fox—
                    they're in a desert
and she's a desert rat.

                    In the mirror
she sees the beginning
                    of the full moon
and more: herself as windstorm,
                    as summer flood,
                    as migrating coyote,
                    as spotted skunk
                         on the run;
                    as sheepherder
                         rounding up strays,
                              cutting cattle
for the Nastacio family ...
          It was the summer her brother taught
her to fly
                    like a bat
(instead of eating
                    the mutton, she fed it
to the wild dogs) and like the other

things
that came while she slept.

"You look like you
just saw a ghost!"
Somebody in the desert
was frying pork chops.
She could smell
the smoke, blue as leaves—at dusk.

He spread the blanket
and made the fire;
she concentrated
on radio static
inside her chest. Once in a while
in it she heard muskrats
and wolves sniffing
the air in the cliffs
above Zuni
where the clans
had their summer
feasts and dances.

The sun,
in her memory,
was going to be her moonlight
all this night long!

II

It gets very cold   here
                in the valley
below Sacred Mountain ...
            Her father proposed
to sell her to a richer family

            ... so she could eat.
"I told him I didn't want to eat."
        So she eats with her fingers,
chili stew ...
The cold made the hunger worse.
            She stood between two
bee-hive shaped ovens
                    in the yard.

In protest her mother
        refused to pack her clothes
so the father had
            to do it himself.
"My grandma told him the BIA
        was against selling children."
Zuni law wasn't
                he said,
against selling.
            She put on her buckskin,
                        moccasins,
ready to go.

The shouting?
               She ran, stumbled—
fell into the catfish-river
    got rear-ended up
the stream, grunting like a Coronado
                        pig,
broken like a Coronado horse,
        the dyes washing
off her skin
    as though she were an olla jar
painted with mudfrogs
               not so carefully
and with the wrong stuff.

III

Stiff, by the light of kerosene,
        on an orange crate,
by a clay pot
    with mudfrogs and delicate
                    plants,
also this—turned the wrong way—
        this arrangement
by the bed...She saw
             a young man looking
      down
up-
    on her, waking.
He said, "Unseen Hands
        placed food before you.
Eat."

Up, back against wall,
the platter of catfish
                on her knees,
still her hunger didn't reach   out
                to it. Of more interest
was the lighted side
        of the wide face
                        above her.
"Who are you?"
                He made his sign,
his fingers, little hapas
        with the corpse-demon heads
you expect.

IV

About the desert,
                she whispered
like a Ramah Mormon peeking
                        into folded hands.
    Not from the terrace
of an old house, not by a fire-
                        place
while using frybread
                as a spoon in stew
or a wrapping for the catfish,
                her father...
about this desert—the opposite
        of "my people lost in the lake"—
    she whispered in a clearing
halfway between Saint John's
                and Surprise Valley,

as though she actually stood
    at a juncture between
the Colorado River and
          the Zuni River north
             of Hunt,
smelling brush burning but
        with no sight
of Sacred Lake. Nothing about this
           desert
reminded her of tomatoes melons
         and peppers.
She whispered with awe
feeling herself sinking in sand,
     as in
water, dying, consumed...
        Thought about guilt,
poverty—
    of the ancient ones, all those
hundreds, hundreds of measured time,
          coming
down from The mesa
       (for no clear reason,
as they had gone up for none).
    If the infants became too
troublesome, why
       wouldn't the ancient ones
          drop
them in a lake? ("In our belief
  these children who *fell*
in the lake
    became the first kachinas.")
They live down at
      the bottom, and come

up at night   and dance:
      in the plaza.
Not always friendly, these—
     You could be left
a bleeding victim of one's rage!

Which way, this Sacred Lake?
At Dowa Yallane it was never mentioned.
Nothing about it and nothing
      about the desert either...

but it goes on: memory, sound
  all of it, the scrapings
on wood, the turnings, Moonlight?
Sun!
The help of Unseen Hands,
      seeing a way through
windstorms, all of it!

Out here, one needed to learn
      to be as untrusting
as the coyotes. Yes,
   moving the way they move;
        carefully.

In Hollywood with the Zuni God of War

"...movie people. They all seemed
quite mad." —Peggy Guggenheim

I

"It's as fake as Zuni
            jewelry made in Taiwan,"
I heard him
        tell the director
and that he was Zuni, and to his disgust
in Culver
        City cops called him Chief.
I was playing a mysterious dark role:
                    not a speaking part.
We were in the Cochise movie
        and this is what Zugowa
                    pointed at, as
he spoke.
        Director bit no tongue:
            Do ya wanna wok or not?

An Italian dude played Cochise.
Apache guy on set told director
                    where to go, too.
Nearly got us all fired; set closed.
            Producers came down, frowning.
The script was all
        about the capture of Cochise.
Zugowa and the Apache tried
to point out to the director
        that he should start

with the white men whipping
                               Chief Mangas Coloradas
because that's where Cochise
gets his anger—his motivation!
Talk about motivation in Hollywood!
                Director told us all,
go get laid in Burbank,
        what ya guys want?

           Ya got Studio City by da balls!
     Ya got all the blondes
        in the District hot fa ya
'cause ya got dok skin and ah—
                  Anyway, Coloradas struck
back   and the white men killed him.
   They say the whole
Apache Nation rose
            and this is where Cochise
of the Chiricahua comes in,
         but the director
wasn't interested. He started his movie
with a bunch of anglo cowboys
                galloping
  across
a phony southwestern landscape
raising a cloud of dust
    trying to track down
               Cochise.
Cochise, you see, before the flick
kicks off, has been accused of killing
    little Micky Free
(we never learn that Cochise
              is innocent,
   and later, that he wipes

out forty before capture. You see
        two fall)
I saw Cochise hiding; Zugowa
     said, "there, away in the hills, but
why isn't he holding them off?"
        till he's captured, but
you don't see the army losses, you instead
        suffer like the ache in Big Eyes'
      knuckles when he drew maps
for Coronado.

II

It was during the time when
everybody was hot and bothered
by that Mexican laborer
   who killed this Indian
over a quarter
which the Indian dropped
         in a jukebox
to play an Elvis Presley song,
    in other words—
You know what he said?
    "What ya got against Elvis?"

Zugowa was in one about
         a stagecoach robbery.
I sat on the sideline singing
    about Dat-So-La-Lee, watching,
chewing sage to keep my breath—

blessed pollenway!—Yuccasweet.
All the Indians were wiped out.
    I saw it in L.A. Without prayer-
meal! The audience loved it!

I was in the Tomassa one,
                Zugowa wasn't. I got shot
in the first scene. A daylight person,
        I turned into a Shutsina—
Zugowa was in the Pocahontas
(silly, silly, silly...) thing,
A remake of forties sentiment,
            ("it cannot be helped;
                    we do not have the same
road," Bunzel quoted Lena
                        Zuni.
Yo-a!
        No tcakwaina mana, this
Pocahontas! Break the piki
            in her honor! She was good,
said the anglos, 'cause
            she saved the life
of one of their own. Two? I forget.

"They did not care
            which tribe we came from."
Zugowa swore this was true
    in the name of Awonawilona,
                by his own mili.
We all looked alike.
        Being herded and shot
paid better than oranges in S.D.
                    County,

or the H.D. in Arizona—that is,
 if you could get yourself shot
at least once
    per month.
A liberal producer
 from back east wanted to make
a flick on Cherokee Gatumlati till
 somebody told him she was half
Negro. Studio pulled the plug
  out of his oxygen tent:
  white audiences in the South
might not buy it.

You might think that because Hopoekaw
    was married to a French officer
she was safe territory, but—

    Hooooooooo thlaiaaaa!

Me and Zugowa tried to get the director
  to eat etawa and yepna.
He left our table gagging.
  Heads in the cafeteria turned,
faces turned red.

We offered him queens,
    Cofachiqui and Pamunkey
 and royalty—Adell C.,
and twisted the arm of Joe Tipp,
  the token,
    but got back "how
many times" etc., and the business

about "point-of-view"
and audience demands.
"Flick like that won't fly!"

III

...and this Navajo hombre said
                              why
         did the Navajo
need a Bilagaana—must have
            been Kit Carson's face!
         or did your ancestors screw
that many blue-eyed settlers?
                    and the black gods?
What's with the black gods—
                        Bitsiislizhims?
         And you say we shot down
our black savior!
            He was no savior, Saiya!
                    You drink too much!

...and he said, We had Yellow Body.
         Calling God.
         Toninili.
         Water Sprinkler.
Zugowa had a friend at Saint Anthony's
                    whose name was Bilagaana.
Imagine that! Know nothing
         about Blue Body. You keep thinking
            "me" some kinda studio-lot-priest!

(...bartender is sympathetic.)
Ahhh, the curse of Haashcheeshzini
                    is henceforth upon you!
"Ready?"
          "Yes, yes! Altseasdzaa!"

IV

Ooooaaaioooo!
          Hoootaa hoooota!
                    ...the movie about Sacajawea,
the so-called Bird-Woman of the Shoshones.
          You
know the story. Ya know it?

"—but they [Lewis and Clark] would
          have lost their direction
                    without a compass."

Mother of Chief Quahhah,
                    Cynthia Ann Parker,
of the Comanches—was proposed
          to the director by a group
of intelligent feminists. He shaved
          his finger at them.
They got the point.

Zugowa and me farmed out
                    parking cars in South

L.A. when the Emily-thing
                        got the okay
from the lot office.
            This jerk-off lieutenant
who's obviously been pumping her,
            marries a girl of the garrison.
Poor Emily, poor, poor Emily!
Emily, the stupid Indian
        "gal" who's shot by a sentry
as she sneaks back
   to warn the garrison of a planned
                        Indian attack.
Last straw!
        The director told us
we were fools to
            jockey autos for peanuts
and tips from the crust! when
                we could ride high
        in the saddle under the big sky!

Some Observations of a Stranger at Zuni in the Latter Part of the Century

I

A stranger to the desert, I come here
with a jaw jammed shut so that speech
comes out like fish falling from a net.
Having chosen Zuni leaves no darkness
roaring in the ears. The decision is
                              ...a sharp fin:
  We enter not by road alone. If, during the trip
  inward—in an unending switch-system as
              on a train rail—the upperbody
  tumbles over a top-heavy house, do not
  be alarmed. We are approaching the end
              of the century, yet Kothluellakwin
  is where Salimopiya will continue
              to carry his yucca switches
and whistle through his blue snout.
I will be his escort between the parked
              Fords and pickups. The dogs leap
                              —leap fast at him!
Okay, we have entered. Incest binds
the people together in the color
              of Corn Mountain. Brother
and sister trusting each other's heartbeat,
swim the morningstar as it rises from
Spirit Lake. They are surrounded by
                              ...powerful, powerful
medicine. Medicine men forgive them,

priests hypnotize them as they watch
themselves—reflected—lose focus in the lake.
                   Only where rules are unbreakable
will I break them.
With no reason to fear Unseen Hands or the ancestors
                             Cliff Bullneck
                             Dirty Water
                             Warmsprings
                             the others
"even if you become a priest" (they told her)
                   you will never make the prayersticks
                   or enter the kiva." You'd think she could
With no reason to fear Unseen Hands or the ancestors
                             Cliff Bullneck
                             Dirty Water
                             Warmsprings
                             the others
"even if you become a priest [they told her]
                   you will never make the prayersticks
                   or enter the kiva." You'd think she could
have turned to the antelope, the great Star
or Forbidden One. I could not help.
I wrote only her name with a stick in the land,
                             in sand. The stick
turned into a horned serpent.
One of her moccasins was stolen from her feet.
The wolves did not take it.
Spider Woman had no interest in a single moccasin.

In the house
there was a cooking bowl, a stone knife.
In the house
there was a digging stick by the door.

On the porch
there was a firestick and a portable radio.

Those who came out of the suds—
                    Siiwhu
                    Siwa
                    Siiwilu
                    Siyeetsa
being unfamiliar with hard surfaces,
watched the white line in the middle
            of the highway with special care. Nobody
called either of the two girls a squaw.
Those times had passed.

If the head needs to be held up, use hands.
The ears will insist on a certain music.
Our Lady of Guadalupe cannot contain
            the body once it starts shaking.
The Catholic Daughters of America
            probably did not have an extra chair.

You peeped through the parsley-colored maze
at her plumage, peeled back from her
                        shimmering body.
You wanted to seduce her for the seeds,
            in search of calmness; you had no idea
how framed and locked otherwise
                        she was. She remains.
Somewhere between Gallup
and the crow's secret you were right
                    to give up.
You had no claims on the pueblo.
Although your presence was tense

your toes might have well exchanged
                    with your heart or nose. I meant
to say all of this earlier.

I hand her a scarlet flower. The Bow Priest
will not hang me from the beam and beat me.
There are rules, laws within laws.

Yahaaaaheeeeyoohoho
Yahaaaaheeeeyoohoho

Ask me no questions—tell you no lies: Spanish
word Zuni is a questionable corruption
        of the Zuni "Shiwi." Pueblo's Keresan.
It sounds like Chinese and can't be linked
        comfortably with any others.
The Slavic shopowners sell junk.
The tourists buy junk.
The paddy wagons pick up drunk Indians
                    ...in Gallup.
The customers of the Indian prostitutes
        are rednecks Mexicans and Others.

She told me early that sheepherding
and silverwork were in their blood. I said how
                    long. It
didn't matter. Her own jewelry was hammered
out of her ancestor's flesh and bones.

In his red pickup, Ciwanakwa waited behind
                    the big rock at Yellow Rock.
He kept his bedding a Sack of Flower Place
because the lone girls came there

to fill the family jugs
with clear, Spring water.
She grew up weary of errands.

She told me about being the Rat Girl singing
in the silence of her own mind, in fear
of the owl. She said
she was always among the Hawikn, shaking the gourds,
insisting on support.
They gave her oxfords—shoes—when
she graduated high school.
At Hawikuh she sang and listened to the echo
of her voice: bouncing
back from the rocks. She said the Crane
Mother protected her there.
The Great Turtle who declared a truce
with Coyote, also
held her hand. I held her hand in dusk-light.
Thin dust rose in red sunlight
as the sun sank into sacred earth: the belly
of a starving child. First Plaza
where kachinas dance in darkness, when
they come back to touch the people.
She feared her own footprints: they might trace
her steps. She could hear
their hearts beating in her ears.
The dwellers woke.
The warriors tipped out of shadows.
They ran—they ran they ran—when they saw
the Ghost Dancer! dancing
and they came back only when
he (her brother) took off his Ghost Dancer-mask.
They swore witchery was in the air.

Women locked windows.
Menfolk went to the kiva to pray.
Even if it was a joke it was not funny.

II

Goose-bump weather, this.
Blazing-Star Eater stands on the fence
                                    keeping the motorcycle gang out
with her strong sense of The Center of The World:
                                                Here.
Anybody can drive onto the reservation but
                                and this is a big but
people are expected to respect the customs.
You know?
                    I count to four, no, ten not to get angry.

When we gather in the home around the stove
and she says give me an "e"
                                    she is barely noticed
in her unlighted corner.
Only when the fire dies does her singing
                        reach them: with its fire.

The rhythm of bedsprings in the night;
snoring from another direction: her barefeet
                                    on the stone floor...
at the window, the garden in moonlight.
              Will the night-dwelling ancestors
betray her? At Halona, will they boo her,
at Wimia, can they send her back to the center,
at Hampasawan, will they drive her east,

at Hawikuh could they join the farmer and learn
to be useful?
I stop at Heshokta (available from the U.S. Government
Printing Office Only) upon demand, up on
the mesa five miles
to the northwest and up there the ancient ones
question my interest, say, "But you have lived among
the anglos
and your ways are not so different from theirs, how
can—" etc.
She tells me that to respond betrays a Larger content,
that at Kwakinawan, in the south-southeast
the ancient questions are not scornful,
not so narrow, not so culturally bound; there, she says,
the river talks to you. The people of Kechipauan
and Kiakime will greet you—a stranger
whose face is a mirror of their own.
You will not beat your fists against your chest!
in agony!

In the months of her cradleboard she scratched
her way out—could not stand confinement.
She gave her father a toothless grin. Shalako eyes.
First-born, she was a Winter Dancer
from the beginning.

III

Not only did she always want
her own way, she had it. In Kothuluellakwin
the question of physical location
     was resolved—in the novel. You
read that? Those words on the seal:
        Ulohnan, Do: Shonan
         Udeman Dehya' A:
       Deyaye
not found over the entrance
             to the underground
                 city
But never mind, the city went
beyond the words.
I had to make my story thrilling
         or die: you
see: the Bow Priest had me hung
up-side-down from a beam
in the roofless old church: I had
no choice but to give it to him
     like he never had it before:
as beautiful as the Chicago shoreline
           at night
all lit up and pretty as snake colors.
They wouldn't let her watch.
Fear, you know, fear she might
     witch them, break their spirits.
You see, the priest had councilmen,
       men with clubs waiting
turns. I was more beautiful than the great
       birds dancing in the dusk.
They cut me down before morning.

The rabbit fur around Nawisho's neck
scared her. This Hehea face
      couldn't be taken in hand, easily.
When they found out she feared it,
      they sicked it on her, Sickum boy!
She stood slightly behind her mother.
Nadir in his darkness showed no darkness.
She refused to hide in her mother's dress.
This was before my time: but related.
Below, in the last light, Hemishikwe
      danced with Nawisho, calling
            rain down.

Not even feathers scared her as much.
Awesome Uwannami danced for thunder.
She got lost running
      in his zigzig. His face:
a mass of clouds, head covered
    with clouds. The butt-feathers?
plucked from a chicken.
Kwelele danced. His gray face,
          white lightning

shooting down, down
and the laughter he inspired spilled
    over into that given to mudheads,
stumbling along the walls of Sacred Plaza.

Her father was a Pautiwa dancer
    that year. She liked his big dog-ears
and the long feathers jutting
    from his head. If only—oh, never
mind. She knew who was inside.

At Shalako—she wasn't the only
    thrilled runner fascinated and
driven. They came out the dressing-house.
Six. Sayatasha, Hutut—two Yamuhaktos,
Salimopiyas—two of these too.
Danced briefly. Shook rattles.
Made bird sounds.
The alternate dancers stored
     their energy for the long night
to come. The bee-hive oven
    was a good thing behind
which to hide. Only thing: as each
bird was escorted you couldn't go
in six directions at once
            to watch
each one stoop to be led
    into the bright electric
lighted house of some newness.

You followed the sound of no more
    than one wooden beak, clacking.
It was no doubt cold, December-cold.
You remembered summer and hammering
    done on the houses. Shirtless
young men sweating over boards
or electricity wires drooping
            from roofs.
Tar paper, too. Or new bricks, new
    plaster or window-frame.
Perhaps from your father's shoulder
you see through the window
    of the house chosen.
     Salimopiya with yucca

switches and fun in his movement...
You wanted to test the pipe-nose.
The big lighted room (framed)
    by the window: glowed—full
of dancing giant birds!
Salimopiya's yellow topknots
      and his blue snout led the eye.
Mudheads danced along the sides
      inches from the feet
of the seated spectators
            with backs
to walls. The drums went on,
            and on, on...
so continuous (you were tranced).

This particular house
      was Sayatasha's—Great Rain Maker
in black and white gown. He came
to the window and spoke
through glass, wishing you Good Health.
Calculated move-
           ments of dignity and grace:
all week, each night all through
      each night, each step
was a spoken thing—something perfectly
designed to drum up something else.
This, by the way, ya know,
      was not the Yaaya.
At this time there was only talk
      of reviving it.

IV

Scuffed oxfords: the hands of Mother.
Pretty Sayastasa belt made to pay
    for those shoes because grades—good
ones were important: and good. I'm learning.
A girl's place was in the home?
      Yahaaaaaaaaaaaaaaheeeeeeeyoooohoho!
      Ya—
Self-disgust gave her a fantasy.
She put on a mask—comedian mask: it
    was like entering...entering
a different point-of-view:
not a Sioux winktas—one a little less
    complicated: wearing a dress
for this one was culturally expected.

Gossip lasted and rested heavily
    in her; men bled their lizzards, it
was no fun knowing the difference
between an irrigation ditch
    a particular way
of looking at something—rear-tip
    feathers, for example.

Rage is a container: it is made.
She feared it would come
    to claim her, bitterly.
"Oh give me a home—"

V

She hears kachinas coming up the ladder.
      The first is Pautiwa, the chief
kachina priest. She screams in his blue
                      face.
As he has his way with her, one
      of his macaw tail-feathers
falls out. Meanwhile, the other kachinas
come up from "where the deer
            and the antelope play"
—an area they crossed coming
            from the suds.
Pautiwa throws her to them
         and they huff
and they puff
at her till there is little doubt
she will give birth to a god.
One makes a cradleboard,
         places it
in her lap, before he hops away;
another takes foodstuff
      from his bag and feeds her.
Others begin dancing and shrieking,
        making the oku call.
Soon, they all are dancing. This
    is when she makes her escape
to "where the buffalo roam,"
        and on beyond to Water's End.
Villagers intent on reviving
        the Yaaya Dance
interrupt her labor
    and take her back to the village

where the kachinas are still dancing, now
in the Plaza—around a little evergreen.
Heshokta-folk pull her into the dance
She escapes again.

Leaving the village, she encounters
                three roads.
She takes the middle. It's a guess.
It leads to Rat Place. Dogs follow her.
One snaps repeatedly at her bare feet.
Going across a yard she rouses roosting
                                turkeys.
The he-turkey calls out to her.
He wants her protection. She has no time.
        And this is not the way back
to Water's End. Given another choice
she would go elsewhere.
She calls out for help.
                A blackbird comes
and perches himself on her shoulder.
He directs her back
                to Water's End.
Just before they reach the place
                        of shame
the bird flies off and away.

VI

They told her to empty the chamberpot,
to fill the terra-cotta jug,
to tend the hogs in the hogshed,
to roll up the reed mat,
to rub the spindle legs of the old,
to tell the little children stories
                         of Zuni glory,
of Ground Rat, Mouse, Owl, Horned Toad,
      Mole, Prairie Dog, Porcupine, Skunk,
Deer Youth, Bear Wife, Mexican, Cloud
                                    Swallower
and War. Then stories of Housebuilding
            and Planting and Weaving.
Later, she was made to tell
                    Santu stories.
            "O Lord Grant Unto Them
            Eternal Rest"

Aashiwi. Because it was habit,
                         she fasted, not
fully believing in its flesh.
She had to be careful: they said,
    there was only twenty-five thousand
                              in the race.
Kyaklo's instructions...

VII

Right in church they deliver
               the Little Doll
from the Big Doll
       but it doesn't matter in
their terms (I speak as an Outsider)
because this Ceremony is not Sacred
             since it is Catholic
and the people left a long time ago.
The Little Doll says to the Big Doll:
          'I'm gonna go to Acoma'
            and she goes.
Wewha the He-She waves goodbye,
       an outsider himself—they
put him in pants and buried him
         wisely as the man he was. 1896.
Half-breeds, too, waved goodbye.
      An old Indian at Crownpoint saw
        her heading for Acoma.
When she squatted
      on the roadside to relieve herself
all the tourists came out with cameras.
The Mormons over at Ramah sent
            their good wishes. She
      was delighted to make new friends.
She wrote to the Little Doll,
      telling her how concerned
everybody had been. Because everything
was going so well, they didn't expect
      any crooked horse-buyers from California
this year. One year we sold them one
         to eighteen dollars

a head. Everything happened in the history
and shadow of Vanderwagen: sheep
for credit.

Imagine an old man chanting
to Uwanammi for rain.
He foams at the mouth.
Imitate Shumeekuli
imitate the Horned One
imitate Shumeekuli
You are at the center of the sixteen
directions
kneeling on your blanket
on top of a mesa,
your jewels and other
worldly possessions on the ground
by your knee
in a Maxwell House Coffee can.
Down below, in the valley,
"Whoopee ti yi yo, get along little,
little dogie"
sounds familiar like
irregular breathing through scar-tissue.
Since you have not declared
a semkonikya beginning
to this prayer, there will not be
a kenkia ending.
You will fast
and plan to float in grace
or disgrace over the Sacred Lake
like the spirit
of the dead.
When you go down you may speak

to the family that keeps the dolls,
say "roadblocks between here
                            and Acoma—more
than Carter has pills in his liver"
            leaving the understanding
that the trip might require prayersticks.

Imagine her brother running
                    from the men who
were supposed to whip him
                at his initiation
                            ceremony!
People on roofs laughed bluntly.
Imagine her turning into
                the Little Doll!
What a laugh!

VIII

She cried out at the first sight
                    of Nawisho, with his
rounded head of buckskin
                        planted
in a bed of turkey feathers,
        the abstracted deer painted
                            on his face
facing the eyes (such eyes)
        and the two vertical lines
                            of thunder
which meant rain.

He, like Hemishikwe, was
                        supposed

to be pretty, a pretty god,
                    good gods both,
gods of fruitlessness.

The old folks teased her
                    about her crying
on sight of mudheads (dark
          with white markings,
zigzagging lines and eyeholes
                    rimmed in white).

IX

This is a circle
                with a tiny central circle
                                    sprouting
eight stemmed flowers
                then the hard jagged lines
                                    of a cross
with a square center: it meanders inside stripes.
Vertical swirls dance through
                    geometric triangles
                    frets
                    expanding circles, larger
than the first ones.
Hemishikwe's big square face,
                    with its oblong slits
                                    for eyes
and the bush of feathers
at the lower part...
                Ah, what's the use?
There's Nawisho—this is his circle, too!

X

She sews me to her bosom,
she wears me sewn
                    with the long thread
of her thought. She'll wear me everywhere
                              with pride.

She weaves the same kind of spell
                    for the others.
Unseen Hands protect her, pour her coffee,
                         make her bed.
Winter flashlights are waved
                    on the roads
in the dark. Her brown legs cast
                    long shadows.
Unseen Hands hold the instruments.
I'm helping her smoothly, coming
     close: she's wearing the Kokokci mask.
I place the Upikaiapona over it.
     She reaches into my shadows.
My struggle is a dance.
I place the Tcakwena over the Upikaiapona.
                              Heavy face!
I go and get the Muluktaka
               and place it over the Tcakwaina.
How many masks can a person's face hold?

I put the Pawtiwa on her next.
                    Heavy, heavy
face: cold act. I wear earmuffs
     and gloves; have trouble keeping my blanket
around my shoulders. She, on the other hand,

is warm—at least in the face.
I hold on to the thread of her thought.

The Hopis stole Cholawitze
                    but he still brings fire
here. We are warm tonight because of it.
I never argue with drunk men:
          they think they are warm
when they are cold
The jukebox was pretty loud—but that's
                              Gallup—yup!

XI

You watch the old man coming
              up the dirt road. He's coughing
a smoker's cough.
                    Traditional headband
around his head; beads around his neck.
Baggy, dirty wool pants, although it's summer,
          hanging halfway
off.
He carries a folded blanket
              balanced on his right shoulder.
When he reaches the point
                    in the road
where you are standing you see his profile,
he turns and looks directly at you,
              no,
through you: tuna pikwayi!
                    Who is he—what does he—?

Yellow coyote eyes: they are flashlights.
You ask.
He tells you he has come a long way
                    to help you:
to prevent tununu—which is when the earth
                    shakes
and splits open and birds fly backwards
                    and horses break their legs
                    running
and houses fall apart
                    and people die in pueblo
                                        rubble
by the thousands. Koli, he says,
                    is his name.

Somebody in the family was expected to die.
She told me to wear a velvet shirt
        and a large western belt
with a silver buckle, jeans and cowboy boots.
She came in buckskin.
The earth was shaking
                    but nobody thought it
                                        serious
enough to panic.
Gravediggers had already dug the graves.
Church bells were ringing.
A burial blanket lay across the back
                    of the couch.
Although it was summer, a fire
                    roared in the stove.
In the yard, her brother
        was swallowing his first sword.
If he pulled it out without sign

of blood,
they would let him in-
            to the Wood Fraternity.
Who was sick?

XII

She now had nightmares
            about being dressed
in white leather—skirt
in blue leather—armbands
in blue leather—helmet-mask
            and blue necklace
and armbands again and wrists
      and knee-decorations:
            trappings!

She watched the older girls
      dance the Kiowa hoop dance
through butterfly eyeholes.

Don't go to the rodeo,
don't go to the parade!

She watched from the shade
            of her shawl:
the saffron one. She first wore it,
      she told me,
when she danced with the girls
      in the dance for Achiyalatopa.

All of this was in the past:
>thank God or somebody! She danced
that winter in her black dress
>>and wore lots of
>>>strung coral,
silver beads and turquoise
>around her neck
>>and on her ears
and wrists and fingers
>and felt fabulous!
It was the winter she began
>to feel like a woman.

XIII

This to string music!
>Huh huh huh huh huh huhhuh!
I help her sing to Muluktaka and Nawisho
>and of poor Cumte'Kaia
>>and the sadness of
>>>Mokwanosana
and to snowflakes and Yamuhakto
>with his armful of wood and
to "The Old Dance Man," Koyyemshi,
to the "Owner of the Springs," Tkianilona!
>This—my chant!
>A ha a ha
>a ha

but sadness is part of what I know.

       Look, I can dance them all,
all—the tricky friend,
       sad. The silly suitor. Sad,
sad—the miracle in the cave,
                          ice cave!
taming of the mountain lion!
          the three virgins!
horror of the wound puttees!
               land-grabbers—!

Keep the music coming!
                 The chanting and the singing
and the dancing, the sad music of joy!

Let the earth burn
       with the intelligence and brilliance
                          of the sun.

We were no longer living
in prehistoric times, I sadly said.
She had said as much many times.
          Laselute
          Laiiuaitsailu
          Patrico Pino
          Palowahtiwa
                    Yo-a! All good
and well, but—
this was the twentieth century (as
   if that meant something profound!)

She said they had a story
          for every occasion:
the unappreciated wife,

the witch whose powers have been confused
                with those of a priest,
how Navajos caused albinos
                        among them. And there was
black Esteban—making Zuni babies
        to the sound of pizzicato notes
somebody from Spain remembered.
        While all this went on,
her telling,
                I imagined glissando runs
sweet enough to taste.

I help her hop
                the snow-bird hop.
She wonders if I'm going to betray her,
        trick her like all the rest.
I hope not. I strut and wobble
        under my helmet-mask. I blow
my bubble gum for her.
        I dog dance,
                        deer dance,
snake dance
                again, hop the snow-bird.
She takes off her dark glasses
        to see me better.
I feel blessed by her Mother of Dawn.
She sings a cowboy song—
        Prince Albert Hunt
    or the Herrington Sisters (I forget
which group). I felt
                protected—yet
distressed   Hoo-o! Ho-o-ota!
                        Lwolohkia-a-a!
O Ko-ko!

XIV

When you eat venison
                    save the fat and bones
for coyote, she said.
If he is not happy, drive him away
with a stick. Turn the logs
            in the winter stove.
One day Turtle says to Coyote,
                "Would you go out
on this limb—?" etc., you know
        The Story:
(The Buzzard took the Monkey
        for a Ride in the Air...)
The Coyote falls
                and breaks his canines.
Say! I remember another one—
                How did Coyote
        get his yellow eyes?
Ahhhhhh. Ya know that one.

You used to listen to Annie Dodge
                    Waineka
    on KGAK in Gallup? The Navajos—
they all said—were out front.
I listened.

When you eat dog meat,
                    don't tell anybody.
There are times when it is necessary.
        When you feel safer attend classes
at the Navajo Community College.
            Shiprock is not far.

Take a flashlight with you
                    if you attend night
classes.   Yo-a!

XV

Frank Darden danced like a god
        and he drove his Thunderbird
with its blue eagle
                    on the hood, the same way.
She thought she loved him, this
Window Rock boy, thought he was a secret hospital
meant to cure her shivers.
                        He worked
as a clerk at a trading post,
his father worked in the coal mines,
mining silver. Frank was tricky: a Navajo,
he wore a T-shirt with the Zuni sign
            of war. He came
barely able to hold the armful of gifts
        he brought for her.
He took her dancing at Window Rock.
He made her think
                    she could win Miss Indian
                        World.
Oiyosoa.
Coupling, said Frank Darden, is
        done the way they bang trains
                            together
in Gallup.
If you are a woman and a Zuni

there are questions to consider:
ways not to be
             one must not be
an ill-mannered tomboy—a tcakwaina mana
a shameless hussy with thoughts
meant for anglos   of genteel-ways
        one must not wear
nightmare leather or give in
        to Pinawa wickedness,
    —no witching around!   —no rock & roll
    —no crazy medicine!   —no hanahha!
If you follow the Old Ways
    and chew the tenatsali
    and wash with the yucca
    and be a good ulani
    and keep a sacred toyallanne
    and keep to one tilinne
    and avoid mosakas
    and keep a sonahtehi life
    and pray—"I sana nakwe..."
If you are a Zuni and a woman
    celebrate ("Ee----------so!")
        the storytelling.

XVI

Kachinas dance around her
        menacing her
with pelts and cedar bark torches.
One
    beats at her bare legs

with yucca switches.
                              She can't put her finger
                  on exactly
what he has done wrong.

Dressed in sagebrush
                  and decorated
with see-through duck feathers, I try
to help,
                  to rescue her. The kachinas
accuse me of trying to imitate
                  Salimopiya.
Sally Mop who? I turn so
                  they can see the hepakine
                                          design
on the inside side of my face.
I flap my parrot feathers
                          in their faces.
I jut my snout at them.
                  They are not impressed.

I go
and sit in a pumpkin patch
                          and sulk.
It's Sunday the fourteenth
    if that means anything.
It's winter too
    if that has any meaning.
Back at the village I can hear them
                                  singing,
and the drums.
They must be planting prayersticks
                  in the Red Earth

Pawtiwa is expected?
           Those with masks wrapped
                       in cloth
have gone to the field
               to dig little holes.
They will place the masks
                  facing east,
in the holes.

              The sun is resting
              on the top
                  of the mountain.

XVII

You dress yourself
             in hawk feathers and wear
                       a halo
of goat's hair around your head.
You decorated your ears with squash
                     blossoms.
You cry raindrops.
You have no idea
     who you are.

You paint your face
             yellow with clay
from the lake. They say
it is Kokokci pink.
Your mirror is not good.

You wear your hair brazenly
    down your back.
They say you must submit
    to flagellations
to drive out the demons.
        You'll feel better.

XVIII

She let her mind wander
    like the line of a blue pencil
tracing a wavering direction on a map
    of the village,
moving along the streets
    and through the yards
        and along the riverbank.

The smoky blue of the sacred mountain
held its own power
    with a stillness
unrelated to its volcanic belly.
    The fire god never slept.
    He could come again
        and burn the villages
          and roll the people
in his ash.

She watched her thought
    follow the movements
made in the Lahewe dance; it moved on
tracing the smell of the hot bread

in the bee-hive-shaped
oven;
on, around and around, inside
the rolled-up cedar bark.

Her line of thought followed the menfolk
out
to sheepcamp, smelled the bacon frying;
the Spring earth,

it cut
like the metal
of skates into the ice
on the frozen lake,

it splashed
and rose and fell like the arms
of the children swimming
in the government-built dam
in August.

XIX

You bring in the firewood,
you go for the food stamps,
you grind the corn, store
the cornmeal in jars
and cook the lamb stew for three days;
then
you bake the bread outside in the oven
and change the tires

on the pickup; you
                    pick up the mail
at the post office;

        and you are careful not to fall
                            asleep
on some mesa and get raped—
                (it happens
all the time)
            because you've seen how
jannis are disgraced—
        whole clans!
                You are careful you stay
away from crevices
                in sandstone—
you know what can suddenly come out!
        so you feed the hogs,
                    feed the chickens,
empty the pee-pot; you know
                    how to be
a good girl.
No way will you give birth to
            an unwanted child, falling
out of the sky, miracle infant
                of some god-awful
                            kachina
(who probably has a secret villa
        in Phoenix—no less).
This way
        you will not have to wear
dark glasses when you go
                    to market
or into Gallup even.

Don't let the boys shake
                their shuminnes
at you. Ignore their bravado.
                    Don't buy
their fetishes—silly ears
        of corn with feathers attached!
They are ready to go
                all the way.
Dressed as Keyemsi such a boy
             can clown his way
into your heart.
            Even the serious ones, like
Kona—with his big yellow head and leopard
                                spots,
can throw you—misdirect you.

Don't get mixed up with the stuck-man
            when you go to Punchkofmoktaqa
to fetch
        berries; he's mystery itself,
a thrower,
            a striped dancer with green horns.

Stay away from Owl dancer,
                Mongwa;

and Longbill—he's just as bad,
            wearing his white and red
                      skins
and waving his green feathers.

Avoid at any cost Palakwai,
                the Hawk,

decked out in exotic feathers
                        with headgear
of white and brown feathers,
                                waving
his red-tail at the flower dancers
                            Tsitoto.
Cook beans for your family
                    but don't dance
with the bean-dancer,
                        Pachavuin mana,
fully covered like a family secret
    (but sacred I'm told!) and
it's probably just as well
                        that you stay clear
of the corn dancers too.
Like the cow-bride in black—
                they carry the spirit
of Angwushahaii.

XX

Not so absolute a stranger to the village
                            as to the desert
in general,
            I was able, on occasion,
to surprise her
                with my ability
                            to call all
the shots, plan the dances,
                    talk the talk.
I told her things

                    she never knew—from
            being so close:
Mastof, sober sober Mastof, she never knew.
She had laughed
                    (properly, of course) at
            blue-faced warrior-Qaletaqa, but—
                            fell over the foot
of the buffalo dancer, Mosairu.
Qoqlo?
        another laugh!

                    with good   will.

XXI

These non-road entrance-ways
                    and the things
they lead (have led?) to—
Piptuka swinging his knotted stick,
(though he swings it for the first time
                            just now)
at the ogre, Toson and at Kikwilyaqua
in his white man's clothes, shaking a gourd;
night rooms rimmed in blue smoke
and peppered with the slow bite
            of western voices, of Zunis
dressed as giant birds, falling
through the smoke that rises...
and the mudheads, on purpose, also
                            falling
so we can hear ourselves cry out,

E-lu! He-lu! Hi-ta!
H-o-o awiyeishikia!
The ways do not lead necessarily
into the house or souls or Spirit Lake,
　　　they may make them expedient,
though to sleep off the bad dream
in a root cellar
　　　　　　or in the granary,
will not work.

A Gallup Swill-Hole
or, Cantina Blues

Her words curled before him in spirals.
She told him "They work
a section gang down the street."
She, Sheba, the Navajo,
never spilled beer.
"My folks are of the [censored] clan."
Her words sped in jerk-motions.
She told him "We left
the reservation when I was ten.
I lost my [censored] when I was eleven."
She went to wait on another table.
A guy slapped her big fat bottom.
A bunch of dudes from Black Mesa mine
still in hardhats came in.
He admired the way she handled them.
Her words curled around their heads:
turning them back into farmhands.
She, Sheba, the Navajo,
punched Hank William's "Lonesome Trail."
She took the empties away and
never once let on that she felt
like [censored] every minute here
with these exsheepherders
in McKinley uniforms.

Tewa Victories

The Town Chief fasting for rain,
a procession of singers walking
      from the desert back
up to the mesa with the little wooden
                    man Saint Augustine;
a lone man carrying a cross
slowly,
down from the mesa to the desert;
another planting prayersticks;
one cocking a rifle, one a sack
              on his back—
going out to plant seed, meanwhile,
chewing the root ballafia...

          and the condor comes
down with a lightness
on the roadside, hops to the body
    of the dead skunk.
Something whispers from the crevice
    in the sandstone
five miles up the canyon.

So the story begins
    without a story intended:
just the dislike he knows,
this He.

He now fed a clown piki.

He imitated a woman sweeping

                         a path
for the Mapuride; he broke all
      the rules when he helped the women
make mudcakes and wrap them
                         in cornshucks.
He himself was the Mapurnin.
He handed medicine to the mayor.
He expressed with hands
         and face the agony
of misunderstanding between
                    a reservation cop
and a personator of a kachina.

The laughter was sincere
when he wiggled like Chu,
            the Snake Kachina.

He shook a yellow gourd
      and kept step
in the circular Christmas dance.
In January he joined the Laguna dance,
      wore the evergreen
branches around his hips but

                         the execution
of the eagle
the day after Home Dance
gave him guilt
            he scrubbed furiously
like a dirty hand.

The mayor speaking Tusayan
congratulated him on the room

           he added to the house
his ma and pa still shared.

He gathered berries
        and passed them around.
The people were tiny, stiff
           and grateful.

One year he was kapyo
           coming up
out of the round house kiva,
throwing a spear at a deer, then
he went out and brought the evergreens
        back on his back.

His father weaved the blankets,
   his mother made the clay pots.

He danced himself crazy
       in the Pinitu fertility parade!

When the woman came
     and asked to be whipped,
the mayor chose him to take up the whip.
She was sure his beating
       would drive out her demon.

He decorated the Kekei Virken.

He kept us in stitches
when he became a coyote trying to chew
          a prayerstick
from the ground.

He ate a natoai
      with more dignity
than any other Hopi.
In the foot races
    he ran faster than roadrunner.

He got his friends to help him
    plant thlawashie
in the Painted Desert—to make
an altar of stones
     where the spirits
could live.

On All Souls day
     he went with his old ma
to the graves where she dug
     a hole
at the head of her father's
      and placed in it
a few bread crumbs.

He broke a bowl on his knee;
     left it on his grandfather's
            grave.
Then back up to the mesa.

He made a circle of candles
     stand
around a bowl of corn.
He lighted them, slowly,
      slowly.

He was chosen to take the sack

of corn down into the kiva
of the War Society. He did it well.

Without touching his knees
            to the ground
he buried an ear of corn
                    in gratitude
to the Great Mother: earth.

They all said his Shichu
                    dancing
tore roughly at the wind
        —and that was very,
                    very
good; better than his coming
        up
out of the earth, all alone,
            as Haukabede,
with such an innocent, decayed
                    white face.

He spoke the words
            of the hakuwam
as though it were a cluster
    of hanging yellow flowers!

As Black Eyes
            he did a two-kiva strut!
As Red Eyes
            he disowned
the taffeta a girl pressed
            into his hand.

When he was too old to play
                    Aiyayaode,
he taught his son;
        except the part where
your cock is supposed to leap out,
                innocently, of
                            course;
bouncing from one thigh
            to the other.
He liked his son best
                as a Thliwa
                        dancer.

On the first deer hunt
            his son experienced,
he taught the boy how to chew
    a piece of venison and suck
in the breath of the dead deer.
He was the Hunt Chief.
            He carried a wolf fetish,
and dreamed all day
                of rabbit stew.

As the Clown, he carried the willow
                            limb,
red as Red Eye's eyes, running
            holding up his yellow limb.

He taught his son
                how to use the figurines
in his wolf pouch; to smoke
out the rabbits hiding
                    in the desert brush;
to throw the koa at the fleeing rabbit.

All his life all was well
                till his wife died
and he could not find another
                          young one.
When he went to an old one
                  for her yes
she told him to get lost.

Sign Language

Lift your left hand
like this. Higher.
That's right.
Keep the fingers tightly linked.
Palm down.
This informs the world
that you are not afraid of flying.
Now, interlock the fingers.
This motion commands
the universe: it means
life is life. Okay?
Beat the palm of the left
hand against the right.
No, harder. Like this!
You know what this means.
This time, hold a level hand
flat against one eye. Yeah.
Look sharply out
of the free one. Get it?
Learn to sleep
with your gloves on. Make sure
the fingers can move
within. Wiggle them.
Keep them warm in this way
all winter. In the spring,
give the gloves to a hawk.
Somebody else will need them.

Glossary

Note: all words are Zuni except where indicated.

Aashiwi: Zuni; the people
Achiyalatopa: kachina of the Sword Swallowers ceremony
                 which takes place every four years in winter
Ahaiyuta and Matsailema: (also Ua nam atch Piahk'oa) sacred
                 and terrible two or twin boys
ah! ahi!: my poor old legs
Aiyayaode: Hopi kachina
akyu: he went
akzeki: boy (very small)
a'lemo ca'lako: grandson!
aliksai (Hopi): once upon a time
anelhaawa: hawk
'a-sh'i-k'-ya: dead
Ash Way: Milky Way
at-e-ya-ye: here are some beautiful flowers
atiikya: dear me! (interjection)
awithluiane: terrace or sacred terrace; the earth (symbol)
                 as sacred altar for use by the gods
awokana-we (male speaking): to all his sisters as group
Awonawilona: Zuni Supreme Being
a-ya-vwi: dangerously susceptible, tender, delicate

Beliciana: Navajo word for Americans

chale: child, or the young of an animal
como los Zuni: when in Zuni do as the Zuni
coral direction: old term for "south"
Cumte' Kaia: father of legendary girl who is raped by
                 kachinas

Ee-e-e-e-so: audience response to storytelling
ele: girl
e'-lu: "how delightful"
E-lu-ya: beautiful ones
esonoteatu: surely or okay
Etawa: turtle

Ha ha waha!: laughter
Hana'hha (interjection): Wow! God! Shit! Damn! etc.
Ha-pa: ghost or corpse-demon
Haukabede: Hopi kachina
Hawikuh or Hawiku: Zuni or Cibola
hehea: wild men of sacred dance, runners to the priest clowns;
        type of face Nawisho has
he'-lu: hurrah!
Hemishikwe: ceremony and kachina
hepakine: Zuni design
him: a suppressed giggle
Hi-ta!: Listen!
Hokuwam: Hopi prayer
Honayane: ritual killing of an eagle
Ho-o-ota! Ho-o-ota!: Come quick! Help!
Ho-o-o-awiyeishikia!: cry of victory
Hoo-o! Lwolohikia-a-a!: Murder! Murder!
Ho-o-o-o thlaia-a!: cry of distress
Huututu: kachina; deputy of Long Horn

ikina: youngest sister
ishanatakyapon: slick, slimy rocks
I-thlim-na: god or superior being

janni: younger siblings regardless of sex

kaka: order of the Sacred Drama; a dance; mother's brother

ka'kamo: Host: Uncle!

ka'semo ca'lako: Nephew!

kawa: oldest sister

kaziki: small girl

kechu (Hopi): animal figurine

Kekei Virken (Hopi): Virgin Mary

kesshe: hello or hi

ketchipawe: calcareous sandstone

Keyemsi: kachinakia-al-lan: water-shield

Kiakima: extinct place at Zuni Pueblo

kirtle: (English)sash to cover genitals and buttocks

koa: throwing stick (Hopi, Pueblos generally)

Koh-thlou-wah-al-wah: ceremony every four years to give
thanks to the kachinas for freedom from
drought and infertility

koko: spirit

Kokokci: kachina of good or beauty

komnin: notched-stick player (Hopi)

Koli: kachina of earthquakes

Kothluellakwin: City of the Kachinas (gods)

Koyyemshi: kachina

kuku: father's sister

kuri: buttocks

Kwarupor (Hopi): movement of dancers toward the kiva after
the Uwepor dance

Kyaklo: kachina priest

Lahewe: one-day corn dance

le-pa-lo-k'ia: food—a red meat paste wrapped in corn husks

Lii thlaia-a!: Here!

lolomai: Hopi word for "hello"

Long Horn: kachina priest

makki: woman, girl

mapurnin: (Hopi) boy in a foot race

mapuride: (Hopi) women who sweep path for foot race

mastof: kachina

metate: mealing-stone for processing corn

mewishokkwa: owl

mili: "Breath of Life"

mi-li-a-me: corn baked and boiled on the cob; dumplings;
griddle cakes

mitsipoca: a dwarf

mi-we: corn on the cob

Mokwanosana: the twins who protect the Zuni; Great Lying
Star—it rises in summer and as early as
midnight foretells of the coming of morning

Mongwa: winged, sacred kachina figure

mosaki: baldheaded man

Muluktaka: ceremonial mask, kachina

Muwaiye: Sword Swallower's dance

na'namo: Host: Grandfather!

Na-ti tsa: meat of the deer

natoai (Hopi): prayerstick

natoypor (Hopi): dancer's altar

Nawisho: ceremony, a Kachina

NCAI: National Congress of American Indians

Neweekwe: Clown Society

Nicotiana attenuata: wild tobacco

O ai o!: I knew it!

OEO (at Zuni): Office of Equal Opportunity

olla: a type of milk

Olla Maiden Dance: civil dance open to public; done by the
traditional Olla Maidens of Zuni

o'-lu-tsi-na: very fine cornmeal
o'-we: fine cornmeal

Palakwai: hawk kachina
papa: older brother
pa'pamo: Host: Elder brother!
Pawtiwa: chief kachina priest; has blue face, blue beak, furry
        ears
peeny: penis
pi-a-la-we: cord or cotton shields
piki (Hopi): type of bread
pinitu (Hopi): spruce
poitaka (Hopi): eye man or tihikya (doctor)
Pollenway: life
Punchkofmoktaga: extinct Zuni place
Qalentaga: warrior kachina

Salimopiya: kachina
sa'-ko-we: mish-yeast (leaven); coarse cornmeal
sawanikia: to "see" an enemy is to take his life
semanawa: to call
semkonikya: the end, thus ends my story, etc.
Shalako: famous Zuni winter ceremony
shi-po-lo-a: mist-enshrouded
shi-u-na: hazy, steam-growing
shohkoya: playing a flute
Shoyakoshkwe: southeastern mesa at Zuni
shuminne: penis (also tu'linne, tilinne, peeny)
shu-tsina: turkey vulture
Siuiuki: a demon (killed by Coyote)
son'ahchi: once upon a time, thus begins the story
sonahtehi: let us follow the ways of our ancestors
sontiinoo: long ago

Soyal (Hopi): house blessing ceremony
sumkup (Hopi): painted buckskin
suwa: younger brother
su'wemo ca'lako: younger brother!

ta'-a or a'-ta-a: corn (generic term)
tada: father or father's brother (uncle) (also tachchu)
talaaaaa: sound made climbing a ladder fast
talaki: males
ta'lemo ca'lako: son!
ta'tcumo: host; father!
tcakwaina mana: ill-mannered girl, tomboy, shameless woman
                (a Hopi expression commonly used at Zuni)
Tcakwena: ceremonial mask
tchu-kwe: silence
tecamika: echo, echo man
tenatsali flowers: medicinal flowers (yellow and blue)
tenkia: the end, it is all, etc.
tesese: "sound of pottery drum, a large jar with skin stretched
        over its orifice" (Tedlock)
thlawashie (Hopi): prayer feathers
Thlim-nah-na: god or superior being
tisshomahha: (interjection) God! Wow! Hell! Shit!
Tkianilona: kachina
to'clemo: great-grandfather
toshiya: so you've come
Towayalanne: Corn Mountain, Thunder Mountain
toyallanne: vagina
tsillu: mother's younger sister
tsitta-lucci: old mother; sister older than mother
tsitta-ts'anna: little mother; sister younger than mother
tuna pikwayi: look through or look fast
tungwayane (Hopi): ritual naming of the baby before the sun
                with prayermeal

Tusayan: Hopi language

ulani: females
Upikaiap'ona: ceremonial mask, kachina
u'wakamo ca'lako: great grandfather!

wavy: crazy

Yaaya Dance: partly a social dance done around evergreen tree
                at plaza center; revived in 1969 after 20 years
                absence
Yamnhakto: kachina
yepna: substance of flesh such as dried meat
Yo-a!: What a pity!
yucca suds: soap

zawaki: boy (older)
zitta: mother

New American Poetry (NAP)

1   *Fair Realism*, By Barbara Guest ($13.95, cloth)
2   *Some Observations of a Stranger at Zuni*, by Clarence Major

Forthcoming:

3   *The Europe of Trusts*, by Susan Howe
4   *A Shelf in Woop's Clothing*, by Mac Wellman
5   *Pieces 'O Six*, by Jackson Mac Low
6   *A World*, by Dennis Phillips
7   *Loop*, by John Taggart
8   *Sound As Thought: Poems 1982-1984*, by Clark Coolidge
9   *Selected Early Poems*, by David Antin

Other books of poetry and poetics available from Sun & Moon Press

From Off the Corner to On the Corner, by Tina Darragh ($4.00, paper)
In Case, by James Sherry ($3.95, paper)
Longwalks, by James Wine ($5.95, paper)
The Travelogues, by Peter Frank ($4.95, paper)
Oracle Night, by Michael Brownstein ($6.95, paper)
From Pearl Harbor Day to FDR's Birthday, by Jackson Mac Low ($5.95, paper)
London, by Fiona Templeton ($5.95, paper)
Methods of Birth Control, by Lewis Warsh ($5.95, paper)
Spoke, by Hannah Weiner ($6.95, paper)
This Is Not a Letter, by Kay Boyle ($9.95, cloth)
Content's Dream: Essays 1975-1984, by Charles Bernstein ($11.95, paper; $16.95, cloth)
Solution Passage: Poems 1978-1981, by Clark Coolidge ($11.95, paper; $18.95, cloth)
River to Rivet; A Poetic Trilogy, by Douglas Messerli ($10.95, boxed set)
Give Em Enough Rope, by Bruce Andrews ($10.95, paper)
The Lives of a Spirit, by Fanny Howe ($10.95, cloth)
Word of Mouth, by Ted Greenwald ($8.95, paper)
The Yellow Floor; Poems: 1978-1983, by Gil Ott ($6.95, paper)
The Sophist, by Charles Bernstein ($11.95, paper; $16.95 cloth)
Poems, by Nick Piombino ($8.95, paper)
My Life, by Lyn Hejinian ($8.95, paper; $12.95, cloth)
Maxims from My Mother's Milk/Hymns to Him: A Dialogue by Douglas Messerli ($8.95, paper; $12.95, cloth)

711   558 -